FROM NICARAGUA, WITH LOVE

Ernesto Cardenal

FROM NICARAGUA WITH LOVE:

POEMS
(1979 – 1986)

Translated & Introduced by
Jonathan Cohen

Pocket Poets Series No. 43

City Lights Books
San Francisco

The translator is grateful to:

The publisher of *Vuelos de Victoria*: Editorial Universitaria, UNAN-León, Nicaragua.

The editors of the following journals, who published some of these translations: *The Agni Review* ("Vision from the Blue Plane-Window," "Founding of the Latin American Association for Human Rights," "The Parrots," "New Ecology," "At the Grave of a Guerrilla"); *The American Voice* ("For Those Dead, Our Dead . . ."); *The Massachusetts Review* ("The Price of Bras").

Cover silkscreen by: Juan Fuentes

CITY LIGHTS BOOKS are edited by Lawrence Ferlinghetti & Nancy J. Peters and published at the City Lights Bookstore, 261 Columbus Avenue, San Francisco, CA 94133

ACKNOWLEDGEMENTS

I wish to express my gratitude to the following friends who helped me in doing this book: Lem Coley, Graham Everett, Hardie St. Martin and David Unger, who offered generous criticism of the translations in manuscript; Daniel Deutsch and David Sheehan, who gave me critical feedback on the introductory essay; my wife, Terry Rosenberg, and my son, Daniel, who both supported my efforts in many ways throughout the project: "What would you think if I sang out of tune . . . Yes I get by with a little help from my friends."

Jonathan Cohen

CONTENTS

INTRODUCTION

Ever since Augustin Videla y Ortiz's "Triste" appeared in Boston's *Atheneum* in 1825, the cry of "tyrants! martyrs!" has been heard in translations of Spanish American poetry. Ernesto Cardenal's poetry echoes this cry for Nicaragua, but more than that, it cries out for a better world, here and now. Unlike Videla y Ortiz, for whom only death offered liberation, Cardenal believes in liberation theology. He believes in the sanctity of revolution: the possibility of "a society of love" in Nicaragua. Indeed, Cardenal's revolutionary politics, first defined in his poetry in the mid-1950s, continue to charge the poems he writes today, and in keeping with his work as Minister of Culture in Nicaragua's Sandinista government, he has further developed in new verse his revolutionary vision.

The poems in this collection represent the latest phase of Cardenal's writing that began with the Sandinista victory in 1979. Most of them appear here for the first time in English. They are not arranged in strict chronological order; rather, they correspond to the thematic development of Cardenal's new work: victory poems, love poems, elegies to Sandinista fighters, travel poems, even a Holocaust poem; socially committed poems reminiscent of the good agitprop written here in the 1930s, such as the New Masses poetry of Muriel Rukeyser, Langston Hughes and Kenneth Fearing; poems of history in the

1

making, in particular, Nicaraguan and U.S. history.

Cardenal says, "I am now writing poetry of a cosmic character, which has elements of mysticism and politics, as well as deeply personal feelings about my life, but it is framed especially in cosmologic language about the problems posed by time and space, matter, the atom, the stars and human evolution." Maintaining that he has always tried to write poetry that people can understand, he notes that since the Sandinista victory, a slight change can be seen in his political poetry: it has become even plainer and simpler than before.

In an essay entitled "Poetry & Politics in Nicaragua," Marc Zimmerman and Ellen Banberger provide valuable insights to the Nicaraguan context of Cardenal's poetry:

> Indeed, since Rubén Darío gave his native nation and area an international standing in literature seemingly out of proportion to its economic and political development, poetry has served as the inscribed mode of culture and counter-cultural expression for those who could write, read, recite, sing, or listen.

> [With] the Sandinista victory of July 1979, an overt political poetry [was]...reborn in the midst of supposedly anti-political modernism, nurtured even in the most reactionary valences of vanguardism, and reaching maturity in anti-Somocista "exterior-ism," burgeoned in the young men and women of

Nicaragua as an essential dimension of a new
counter-culture . . . . Finally, of course, this new
Sandinista culture, so much embodied in poetry and
the song movement which accompanied it and in
fact fed it, would become the basis of the militant
anti-interventionist culture that would develop
throughout the Reconstruction.

Cardenal is the acknowledged master of Sandinista poetry. Taken
out of Nicaragua by way of translation, his work loses the
context of significant elements rooted in the culture of his
homeland. Nonetheless, Cardenal's kinship with North
American poetics allows translations of his poetry to achieve an
almost eerie naturalness in English.

* * *

As my "Note on Translation" says in Cardenal's *With Walker
in Nicaragua*, I work at bearing his utterance into my own. I try
not to produce lifeless literal translations simply to help readers
get through the Spanish texts *en face*, or spirited imitations,
freely adapting Cardenal's poetry to express myself, not him.
Instead, I try to paraphrase him, as if he were originally writing
his poems in English. Like Cardenal, I make use of the natural
rhythms of everyday speech, as well as different levels of diction,
doing my best to put real feeling in the language. I focus on
re-creating in English the tonal structure of his poems, paying

3

special attention to the tonality of each line, and to the poetic effect Cardenal achieves by varying the length of his lines. In sum, to produce an accurate translation as faithful as possible to the letter while maintaining the poetic quality of the original Spanish, I translate sometimes word for word, sometimes sense for sense, rendering not simply what Cardenal says, but what he means, poetically.

I have worked closely with Cardenal in making these translations. During the past year or so he has sent me new poems in manuscript, and suggested others recently published in Spanish, some already translated; for instance, he noted that "New Ecology" was especially well-received throughout his U.S. reading tour in the spring of 1985. From all this material I then selected representative poems for the book. I agreed to retranslate a few poems already available in English (see Cardenal's *Flights of Victory*, edited by Zimmerman) because they deserve another chance in English, another reading and rendering, given the range of possibilities inherent in translation.

Cardenal has carefully reviewed my work, correcting me when I strayed too far from what he means in Spanish. For example, a good deal of "Room 5600," the parts relating facts about the Rockefellers, is based on a chronicle written in English (see *The Rockefellers: An American Dynasty* by Collier and Horowitz). Because the Spanish *cuarto* (room) does not, Cardenal feels, convey the commercial meaning of the word in English, he

4

uses *oficina*. Literal translation creates a mistranslation here. I made this mistake at first, not knowing about the legendary Room 5600 of the Rockefellers, also referred to as the Office. But Cardenal clarified this term for me. In other lines of this poem, when my translation betrayed the source material, Cardenal offered me the original English which I, in turn, worked into the poem.

"New Ecology" provides another example of how Cardenal and I have worked together. This poem uses the common Spanish names of several animals found in Nicaragua. I spent hours in the library trying to find the common names of these animals in English, but *culumucos* escaped me. It appears in the line: *"En la carretera más conejos, culumucos."* I then called the Nicaraguan Embassy, but no one there knew the English name. My friends from Central America didn't either — most had never even heard of *culumucos,* and one could only tell me they were small, furry animals. So I made up "raccoons," faking it like a musician who doesn't know the original melody of a composition, and plays a melody of his own invention based on the harmonic structure. By using "raccoons" in the line — "Along the highway more rabbits, raccoons" — the English would at least be faithful to the alliteration of the Spanish wording, and to the idea behind the line. Although I prefer to paraphrase, rather than imitate, I considered this the best solution to the problem. More would be lost , it seemed to me, by using the Spanish name. Finally, when I proposed my solution to Cardenal, he said that he liked it and authorized it.

*   *   *

Regarding the politics I have translated, I am well aware of the many questions now surrounding the Sandinista Revolution that Cardenal serves in verse: Is it the revolution of love he celebrates here, or yet another revolution of lies and special privileges? Has it become the revolution of sharks? Another revolution of shutting people's mouths? The truth matters to anyone who wants to understand Nicaragua, and to anyone interested in understanding Cardenal as a witness to history. Here are his visions of the revolution in Nicaragua.

Jonathan Cohen

SIGNIFICANT DATES IN CARDENAL'S LIFE
AND LITERARY CAREER

1925   Born in Granada, Nicaragua (January 25).

1930   Moves with his family to León.

1932   Writes first poem he remembers ever writing, an
            homage to Rubén Darío.

1935   Returns to Granada.

1943-1947   Attends University of Mexico, studying literature
            and philosophy; writes thesis entitled "Ansias y
            lengua de la nueva poesía nicaragüense" (Longings
            and Language of the New Nicaraguan Poetry);
            receives degree.

1943-1945   Writes *Carmen y otros poemas (Carmen and Other
            Poems)*, his first collection (still unpublished and,
            according to his wish years later, not to be
            published in his lifetime).

1946   Publishes love poems in Mexican journal; writes
            his first long poem based on history, "Proclama

del conquistador" (The Conquistador's Procla-
mation).

1947-1949   Attends graduate school at Columbia University;
comes under Pound's poetic influence and, most
important, begins to identify himself as a poet.

1949   That spring, writes "Raleigh," the first poem that
represents his mature voice; in the fall goes to
Europe for study and travel.

1950   Returns to Nicaragua (Managua); writes "Con
Walker en Nicaragua" ("With Walker in
Nicaragua"); becomes involved in revolutionary
activities.

1951   Sets up a poetry press called *El hilo azul* (The Blue
Thread) which runs for two years; works with José
Coronel Urtecho on translations of North
American poetry; becomes active as member of an
illegal group of young revolutionaries called
UNAP (National Union of Popular Action).

1952   "Con Walker en Nicaragua" wins prize of the
Managua Centenary; starts writing epigrams
which link subjects of love and politics.

1954	Takes part in failed rebellion (April) against Somoza dictatorship, and leaves Nicaragua for a while — lucky not to be captured, tortured and killed as were several of his close friends.
1954-1956	Writes *"La hora 0"* ("Zero Hour"); coins the name *exteriorismo* for his poetic style; translates epigrams of Catullus and Martial.
1956	Experiences religious conversion (awakening).
1957	Enters Trappist monastery in Kentucky, Our Lady of Gethsemani, and becomes disciple of Thomas Merton, forming bonds of lifelong friendship; exhibits his sculpture at Pan American Union in Washington, D.C.
1959	Publishes *"La hora 0"*; unable to withstand rigors of monastic life, leaves Gethsemani at Merton's suggestion and goes to Benedictine priory in Cuernavaca, Mexico, to study theology.
1960	Publishes *Gethsemani, Ky.* (poetry), written in Cuernavaca; also publishes a translation of Pound's "A Few Don'ts" as *Varios "no"* which serves as an *exteriorista* manifesto.

9

1961-1965	Completes preparation for priesthood in seminary of La Ceja, near Medellín, Colombia.
1961	Publishes *Epigramas: poemas* and a volume of his translations of Merton's poetry.
1963	Publishes book of translations (co-authored with Coronel) of contemporary North American poetry, including work of Merton, Allen Ginsberg, Kenneth Rexroth, Denise Levertov, Gary Snyder, Lawrence Ferlinghetti, Robert Lowell, and others; Merton publishes his Cardenal translations in *Emblems of a Season of Fury*.
1965	Ordained Roman Catholic priest in Managua on August 15, the Feast of the Assumption; publishes *Oración por Marilyn Monroe y otros poemas (Prayer for Marilyn Monroe and Other Poems)*.
1966	Sets up contemplative commune with church in Solentiname, Nicaragua, calling it *Nuestra Señora de Solentiname* (Our Lady of Solentiname); publishes *El estrecho dudoso (The Doubtful Strait)*, a sequence of historical verse-narratives.
1967	Publishes *Salmos (Psalms of Struggle and Liberation;*

also, *Psalms*), written in La Ceja, and two anthologies of his poetry; also publishes his Pound translations (co-authored with Coronel) in *El corno emplumado/The Plumed Horn*.

1968   Thomas Merton dies, accidentally electrocuted in Bangkok (December 10).

1969   Publishes *Homenaje a los Indios Americanos (Homage to the American Indians)*, poems begun in La Ceja and the first to be completed in Solentiname.

1970   Spends three inspirational months in Cuba, experiencing what he later refers to as his "second conversion"; publishes prose meditations entitled *Vida en el amor (To Live Is to Love;* also, *Love)*, written in Cuernavaca, with preface by Merton dated 1966.

1971   Publishes *La hora cero y otros poemas* and three other anthologies of his poetry; *Psalms of Struggle and Liberation* published, translation by Amile G. McAnany; starts correspondence with Jonathan Cohen, reviewing Cohen's translation of his poetry

(*Prayer for Marilyn Monroe and Other Poems*), and encouraging him to work as his translator.

1972   Publishes *En Cuba*, prose account of his trip to Cuba, as well as *Canto Nacional* ("*Nicaraguan Canto*"), dedicated to the FSLN (Sandinista National Liberation Front); *To Live Is to Love* published, translation by Kurt Reinhardt.

1973   Publishes "*Oráculo sobre Managua*" ("*Oracle over Managua*"), his first thoroughly Sandinista poem; *Homage to the American Indians* published, translation by Carlos and Monique Altschul.

1974   *In Cuba* published in translation by Donald D. Walsh; *Love* published, translation by Dinah Livingstone.

1975   Publishes prose work entitled *El Evangelio en Solentiname (The Gospel in Solentiname)*, a collection of recorded dialogues; *Marilyn Monroe, and Other Poems* published, selections translated by Robert Pring-Mill.

1976-1980   *The Gospel in Solentiname* published in four volumes translated by Walsh.

1976	Publishes *La Santidad de la Revolución (The Sanctity of Revolution)*, a volume of prose and poetry.
1977	Our Lady of Solentiname destroyed by Somoza's National Guard in the aftermath of a failed Sandinista uprising in which members of Cardenal's commune had taken part; forced into exile in Costa Rica, from where he serves as roving ambassador for Sandinistas; *Apocalypse and Other Poems* published, a selection of his short poems translated by Merton, Pring-Mill, Rexroth, and Walsh.
1979	Appointed Minister of Culture of Nicaragua, following the Sandinista victory on July 19; establishes Houses of Culture throughout country, and soon people of all walks of life — workers, peasants, soldiers, policemen — are participating in workshops for poetry, drama, music, and painting.
1980	*Zero Hour and Other Documentary Poems* published, selections translated by Paul W. Borgeson, Cohen, Pring-Mill, and Walsh; awarded prestigious Peace Prize of the German Publishers Association

for a canon revealing "love as an essential element of social change."

1981   Publishes *Tocar el cielo (Touching Heaven)*, new poems; *Psalms* published, translation by Thomas Blackburn and others.

1984   *With Walker in Nicaragua and Other Early Poems* (1949-1954), selected and translated by Cohen.

1985   *Vuelos de victoria* (poetry) published in celebration of his 60th birthday — *Flights of Victory*, selections translated by Marc Zimmerman and others; suspended by Vatican for government work, but refusing to "abandon the people," continues as Minister of Culture; gives reading tour in United States, visiting New York to be the featured poet of first Latin American Book Fair.

1986   Continues government work at home and abroad; sends Cohen new poems in manuscript for translation, *From Nicaragua, with Love*.

VISION FROM THE BLUE PLANE-WINDOW

In the round little window, everything is blue,
land bluish, blue-green, blue
                        (and sky)
        everything is blue
blue lake and lagoons
                    blue volcanoes
while farther off the land looks bluer
        blue islands in a blue lake.
This is the face of the land liberated.
And where all the people fought, I think:
                                    for love!
To live without the hatred
                        of exploitation.
To love one another in a beautiful land
so beautiful, not only in itself
                but because of the people in it,
above all because of the people in it.
That's why God gave us this beautiful land
for the society in it.
And in all those blue places they fought, suffered
                for a society of love
                        here in this land.

One patch of blue looks more intense . . .
And I thought I was seeing the sites of all the battles there,
and of all the deaths,
behind that small, round windowpane

                              blue
                    all the shades of blue.

NEW ECOLOGY

In September more coyotes were seen near San Ubaldo.
More alligators, soon after the victory,
        in the rivers, out by San Ubaldo.
                Along the highway more rabbits, raccoons . . .
The bird population has tripled, we're told,
        especially tree ducks.
The noisy tree ducks fly down to swim
                where they see the water shining.

Somoza's people destroyed the lakes, rivers and mountains, too.
        They altered the course of the rivers for their farms.
The Ochomogo had dried up last summer.
The Sinecapa dried up because the big landowners
                                stripped the land.
The Rio Grande in Matagalpa, all dried up, during the war,
        out by the Sébaco Plains.
They put two dams in the Ochomogo,
                and the capitalist chemical wastes
spilled into the Ochomogo and the fish swam around as if drunk.
        The Boaco River loaded with sewage water.
The Moyuá Lagoon had dried up. A Somocist colonel
robbed the lands from peasants, and built a dam.
The Moyuá Lagoon that for centuries had been so beautiful.

(But the little fish will soon return.)
They stripped the land and they dammed the rivers.
    Hardly any iguanas sunning themselves,
                                hardly any armadillos.
Somoza used to sell the green turtle of the Caribbean.
They exported turtle eggs and iguanas by the truckload.
    The loggerhead turtle being wiped out.
José Somoza wiping out the sawfish of the Great Lake.
In danger of extinction the jungle's tiger cat,
    its soft, jungle-colored fur,
and the puma, the tapir in the mountains
        (like the peasants in the mountains).
And poor Rio Chiquito! Its misfortune
the whole country's. Somocism mirrored in its waters.
The Rio Chiquito in León, fed by streams
of sewage, wastes from soap factories and tanneries,
white water from soap factories, and red from tanneries;
plastics on the bottom, chamber pots, rusty iron. Somocism
left us that.
(We will see it clear and pretty again singing toward the sea.)
And into Lake Managua all of Managua's sewage water
and chemical wastes.
    And out by Solentiname, on the island La Zanata:
a great stinking white heap of sawfish skeletons.

But the sawfish and the freshwater shark could finally
                            breathe again.

Tisma is teeming once more with herons
                              reflected in its mirrors.
It has many grackles, tree ducks, kingfishers, teals.
              The plant life has benefited as well.
The armadillos go around very happy with this government.
                  We will save the woodlands, rivers, lagoons.
We're going to decontaminate Lake Managua.
The humans weren't the only ones who longed for liberation.
The whole ecology had been moaning. The Revolution
also belongs to lakes, rivers, trees, animals.

THE PARROTS

My friend Michel is a commanding officer in Somoto,
            near the border with Honduras,
and he told me about finding a shipment of parrots
that were going to be smuggled to the United States
            in order for them to learn to speak English.
There were 186 parrots, and 47 had already died in their cages.
And he took them back to the place from where they'd
                        been taken,
and when the truck was getting close to a place
                        called The Plains
near the mountains where those parrots came from
            (the mountains looked immense behind those plains)
the parrots began to get excited and beat their wings
            and press themselves against the walls of their cages.
And when the cages were opened
they all flew like arrows in the same direction
                        to their mountains.
That's just what the Revolution did with us, I think:
it freed us from cages
            in which we were being carried off to speak English.
It brought us back to the Homeland from which
                        we'd been uprooted.

Comrades in fatigues green as parrots
                        gave the parrots their green mountains.
              But there were 47 dead.

EMPTY SHELVES

Yesterday I went into a supermarket
                     and saw shelves bare-empty;
most of them empty; and I felt a little
of the gloominess of the empty shelves,
    but more than that, the happiness
because of the dignity of our people plain to see
                          on the empty shelves.
These shelves before just overflowing
with luxuries and necessities of all colors
or as they are in other countries. It's the price
we're paying, a small nation fighting
against the Colossus, and I see empty shelves
completely full of heroism.
           The price of independence. And because there are
thousands of Sandino's cubs* loose in the woods.
And just as those rows of colorful things are gone
so is the lady on the sidewalk pointing to her sores,
the little boy with eyes white as marble, holding out his hand.
       The kids are playing in their neighborhoods;
                  the grownups, peaceful.
And the police in the street have no rubber clubs
for beating people,

                    no tear-gas bombs
no water hoses or anti-riot shields
because of these empty shelves.
                         Bare-empty shelves
without necessities or luxuries, but brimming with sacrifice
and pride.
Pride, arrogance if you wish, of a people:
these empty shelves.
                    It's not being sold or surrendered.
And I went out, feeling bad but glad because of
                              the empty shelves.

---

*Cachorros de Sandino, the nickname of young draftees in the Sandinista army, plays on the double meaning of the word *cachorros*: cubs and pistols.

ECONOMIC BRIEF

I'm surprised that I now read
                    with great interest
things like
        the cotton harvest up 25%
from last year's crop
                U.S. $124.2 million worth of coffee exported
        up 17.5% from last year
a 13.6% jump in sugar is expected
                    corn production dropped 5.9%
        gold dropped 10% because
of attacks by the contras in that region
likewise, shellfish . . .
When did these facts ever interest me before?
        It's because now our wealth,
                        meager as it may be,
            is intended
                for everyone.
                        This interest of mine
        is for the people, well,
                out of love
            for the people. The thing is
now these numbers amount to love.
The gold coming out of the earth, solid sun

cut into blocks, will become electric light,
drinking water
                for the poor. The transluscent
mollusks, recalling to mind women, the smell of a woman
coming out of the sea, from their underwater caves
and colorful coral gardens, in order to become
pills, school desks.
                The holiness of matter.
        Momma, you know the value of a glass of milk.
The cotton, soft bit of clouds,
            — we've gone to pick cotton singing
                we've held clouds in our fingers —
will become tin roofs, highways, and
the thing is now what's economic is poetic,
        or rather, with the Revolution
the economy amounts to love.

APPARITION IN HAMBURG

1,000 people listening to my poetry
and 300 in the street, unable to fit in the place
      — you know: the publicity
          the celebrity . . . and the Nicaraguan cause —
all of the faces in the dark (for me)
    the entire audience behind the spotlights,
      a thundering, applauding shadow,
but then in the light, very close to me,
almost on stage, sharing the powerful lighting with me,
I saw you
        short hair, messed up a little,
the girl with eyes the color of muscatel
      or sometimes the ocean's color on the high seas
      or somewhere in between green and soft blue
        (and it was as if the sky were watching me),
    that very same mouth,
      mouth I drank in my mouth,
an 18-year-old girl again,
the same age as 30 years ago,
but German, I suppose, this time,
being able just to sneak looks at her now,
she beside me in my orbit of light,
    in front of the blinding spotlights,

on a bench; after her
some three other girlfriends half in the dark;
and so among something like 1,000 faces
hers was the only one I saw.
Who on earth would ever tell me that you had reappeared,
the one whom the One, capital O, pulled out of my arms,
the girl I let go to embrace the Invisible,
my pretty ex-cherub whom I kissed so much but never enough,
                    mouth I drank
now here again, 30 years later,
                    lips curled slightly
by a smile,
      eyes troubled suddenly by an angelic
sexy feeling,
like that angel full of lust
more so by being made of flesh than by being an angel,
my pretty girl, urchin, whom I embraced
at *"Las Piedrecitas"* under the stars — do you remember? —
whom I embraced in a man's coat,
that coat of mine I lent you for the cold,
whom I left for God,
      sold out for God — did I end up the loser?
I left you for sadness.
            Applause for my verses
            with chants in Spanish
            No Pasaran

27

and I being able just to sneak looks at her.
　　　　Skin like a pale apple's, like
the apple just picked from the tree
that I nibbled on later, that night, in my room at the *Prem* Hotel
tart, sweet, light green, juicy, fleshy
but it was a fruit, and not the other thing.
　　　　　　　No Pasaran
It was as if I were losing her again
as if she were being given to me again and I were giving
　　　　　　　　　　　　　　her up again.

　　　A renunciation that had been hard
　　　　and was still hard, becoming an entire life,
and now the renunciation again,
so fleeting this time,
　　　　　but nonetheless hard, painful,
amid the applause of the shadows,
the pain of feeling that you might be her again
and at the same time, maybe worse, the pain that you weren't.
A German girl, I suppose, who is unaware of all this
the other girl who once resembled you knows about,
　　　　　my baby then 18 years old
　　　　　　　(she knows these lines are for her)
　　　　　on that gloomy Somoza night,
the lights of the dictator's palace
reflecting in the Tiscapa Lagoon.

The one who admired my black hair — do you remember? —
and once you called it "pitch black!"
in that restaurant.
                    The darkness applauded
my poems:
          "their battle hymn was a love song
                    If Adelita . . ."
and I meanwhile so much like our war cripples
paraplegics
peacefully sitting in their wheelchairs.
But there wasn't any bomb.

     There was an anonymous call about a bomb
that the police didn't believe.
We might have died together, my love,
I, a short-lived bit of news in the paper,
          like that short-lived flower of the cortez trees
                    "when the golden cortezes flowered"
                    and you
simply a German girl (I suppose)
with any name.
But the girl who made me give up again the one from before
young and fresh this time just like before
while they were taking up the collection among the crowd,
burlap bags filled with heavy coins and bills;
and some 15,000 marks were raised for the Nicaraguan
                                        people that night.

VISIT TO WEIMAR (GDR)

We were passing through Weimar and naturally
                              we went to Goethe's house.
His paintings were there. A Lucas Cranach . . .
        An Italian primitive . . .
Also a delicate pencil drawing he made
        of his pretty wife asleep in the garden.
The piano where the young Mendelssohn played.
Greek statues, his collection of minerals.
        The desk where he wrote *Faust*.
His poor bed. The armchair where he died.
Very elegant drawing rooms because he was Prime Minister;
                              his bedroom
        modest like Lenin's in the Kremlin.
The couch where he used to spend all night talking
                              with the Prince of Weimar.
"Profound thoughts concerning nature and art."
A time he devoted more to the natural sciences than to poetry.
Here he discovered the intermaxillary bone in man.
Also the vertebrae theory of the skull.
In 1790 he began the study which led to his theory of colors.
(The same year that he wrote *The Metamorphosis of Plants*.)
It was a snowy day when Schiller came to Weimar to live.
        He had a conversation with Napoleon here.

In 1815 he was appointed Prime Minister.
(He was also a kind of Minister of Culture.)
This was the intellectual capital of Germany.
Here young Heine, boasting, told him
that he too was at work writing "his" Faust.
And that the plums in Weimar were so delicious!
The devastating effect that Schiller's death had on him.
The Botanical Garden in Palermo revealed the proto-plant
to him.

Working on *The Metamorphosis of Animals*
he became more and more convinced
that the art of poetry is "a common property of mankind"
and in all times and places it exists in thousands of people.
Poetry writing could be taught to the masses.
All that mattered to him were culture and barbarism, he said.
He was ending up alone.
In 1827 his Charlotte died.
The next year, the Grand Duke.
But he had written: "There is always a quiet in the treetops."
At the end of Book II, Faust, now blind, has the vision
of "a free people living on this earth."
He put a lock on the covers of Book II
and stuck it in a cabinet he locked so that no one could read it.
Later on, he no longer left his room to go into
the elegant drawing rooms.

The day he was dying in his armchair
          he thought he saw a letter from Schiller on the floor.
And 15 minutes from there
                    forests all around
We enter the "Highway of Blood."
          The prisoners themselves paved it.
It ends at deserted platforms.
          where hundreds and hundreds and hundreds of trains
                              used to come.
The imposing bronze doors open for us,
                    with a flowered grille
and big letters backwards, above the grille,
that only can be read inside, once the doors have closed:
          EVERYONE RECEIVES WHAT HE DESERVES
like the entrance to Dante's Inferno
          Lasciate ogni speranza, o voi che entrate
          It's the entrance to Buchenwald.
Barbed-wire fences inside of barbed-wire fences inside
                    of other electrified barbed-wire fences.
          The horrifying turrets.
And we saw the red-brick ovens of the crematorium.
The "special" cells of the ones who resisted,
where before dying heroes cried out
                    from the little hole with bars,
to the whole camp, not to surrender.
It was truly another town.

With as many inhabitants as Weimar.
Their bodies walking skeletons
    a tottering footstep
        a blank stare full of terror.
Everything well planned.
The name of each person who was going to arrive
announced beforehand at the concentration camp
with a copy to the Central Office of Concentration Camps,
cc: Gestapo, etc.

> "In reference to what has previously been
> discussed I enclose in duplicate, for the
> necessary purposes, the list of those unable to
> do work"
> *(Signed)*

        Camp Doctor of Buchenwald.
On the outskirts, mounds of corpses.
The grey building with different floors where they
        left their clothes.
Girls wearing elegant dresses
    came out wearing the blue-and-white striped uniform
with a number tattooed on their left arm
    many soon dying from sheer grief.
Human skin was good for parchment.
    For writing poems on it, romantic ones.
  For binding books.
  For lampshades.

They shrunk Jewish heads (like the Jívaros), for souvenirs.
And doctors doing all kinds of experiments on live bodies.
There were 18-hour workdays in December, out in the snow
                                                    and wind,
          wearing just a thin jacket,
and many were so cold they threw themselves on the
                              barbed-wire to be electrocuted.
The children put in a separate pen
their barbed-wire pen inside of barbed-wire fences
                              inside of more barbed-wires.
Next to them a small barbed-wire cage with bear cubs
          (the children loving those cubs)
and when the children cried from hunger
the guards poured plenty of milk for the bear cubs
          so that the children might see it,
                                        the cute little bears
and the children crying, screaming.
          Floodlights revolving in the fog, revolving,
          searching for a fugitive
and the gruff barking of the police dogs behind
                              the barbed-wire fences
          and its echoes.
One could tell if they were burning corpses in the ovens
if the smoke coming out was black or white.
          And from the delicious smell of roasting meat.

The voice of the pastor admonishing them, gripping the bars
                    in the final cell.
We saw the apparatus "for measuring a prisoner's height"
and the little window behind it that opened up and out
                                    came a hand with a pistol
        to shoot him in the back of the neck.
Before, a "doctor" examined his teeth
                looking for gold.
The fact is they'd discovered the dead bodies yielded money;
Hair, gold teeth, fat, skin for artwork.
                    Capitalist economy to the point of madness.
    "Contents of shipment:
                    2 kilos of hair in locks and braids"
The death trains always pulling up to the platforms.
And in Weimar nobody knew anything.
They only saw a forbidden zone and a long line of trains.
But they got suspicious
when an army truck crashed right in the center of town
and piles of corpses fell onto the street.
        These were the forests where Goethe would go for walks.
Close to here the oak tree that Goethe used to read beneath.
    And that the Nazis took good care of.

A GLASS OF WATER IN COLOGNE

I ask for a glass of water in Cologne
in some restaurant with a view of the
                              greenish-looking Rhine.
Hermann tells me: "The water in Germany is bad.
              It's not like Solentiname's.
                    It's water from toilets."
I try it, he's right.
        Colorless, tasteless and odorless, toilet water
              that's been sterilized.
It has been recycled at least ten times.
It has passed through a human body. Come out with
                              urine and fecal matter.
Been drunk by animals and urinated and defecated by them.
Been purified and sterilized.
        Passed once more through a human body.
Passed once more through toilets and urinals.
Water from hospitals and brothels
running once more through sewers
        to the greatest sewer in the world, namely, the Rhine,
loaded with arsenic, mercury, sulfuric acid,
then purified again.

Put into this glass.
I think about a glass of water from Solentiname,

                                      fallen from the sky.

(*Note:* Solentiname is an archipelago of thirty-eight islands located in the remote southern part of Lake Nicaragua, site of Cardenal's commune and church.)

FOUNDING OF THE LATIN AMERICAN
ASSOCIATION FOR HUMAN RIGHTS

The conference hall shaped like an amphitheater,
                              functional, in
a genuine non-style,
        typical intercontinental architecture,
                    delicately covered
with a rough cream-like material, its texture exciting
                                    to the touch,
and where the dark brown plywood sparkles in the golden light
cast by silver-looking cylinders from the white plastic ceiling
and even more
by the dazzling spotlights, and the flashes from
                              the photographers;
where the row of Latin American flags
is a single blend of national colors without borders
behind the table on stage where the board of directors sits
with bright glasses of bubbling water
and the podium with its chrome microphone gleaming
                              in the spotlights:
this hall in Quito,
        I see it today, from my place on the stage
              strangely, full of animals.
There are ex-presidents. Important personalities.

From the iguana slowly came about this species
that is seated in this conference hall
and from the microphone it denounces fascist regimes.

   Article 16: The Executive Committee has the following duties
We are an animal, each one separate, individuals.

                              An animal just as iguanas are.

   Though we call ourselves a rational animal.
But together we are NOT an animal, we are man:
man, for instance, in this hall, defending man,

                          his human rights.

We are a singular species, with eyeglasses, neckties, hairstyles.
It's taken a lot to come from life in the trees to these proposals.
We are a strange being
looking at each other, smiling at each other, talking to each other
in this hall:

                    a diverse being and one being.

                 In this hall there is only One
in many seats, the person standing up,
another taking out a cigarette,

                          some other photographing the rest.

The Arauacos gave themselves the name,

              Arawak: which means "man"
                       "people."

Ruth Benedict says that the Zunis, the Danés, the Kiowas
gave themselves those names, which mean: "human beings"

                 though they were surrounded by other nations.

The Colombian Koguis: "people" is their name.
                    My Yaruro friends: "people" is their name.
              And in Antioquia, at that Indian boarding school
a young Páez told me the name of his tribe is not Páez but *Naza*
                    "which means people or person."
The animals adapt themselves biologically
to the environment, and their adaptations are hereditary.
                                        (Hence the species.)
Man's adaptations are cultural,
not subject to heredity. Judging by what Paul said:
                    "there's neither Jew nor Greek."
I keep looking at my species for a long time
though the flashes and the spotlights blind me.
Gentlemen: solidarity with Bolivia, with El Salvador
is a human effort that began with our brother the iguana.

"FOR THOSE DEAD, OUR DEAD . . ."

When you get the nomination, the award, the promotion,
think about the ones who died.
When you are at the reception, on the delegation,
                                        on the commission,
think about the ones who died.
When you have won the vote, and the crowd congratulates you,
think about the ones who died.
When you're cheered as you go up to the speaker's platform
                                        with the leaders,
think about the ones who died,
When you're picked up at the airport in the big city,
think about the ones who died.
When it's your turn to talk into the microphone,
                              when the tv cameras focus on you,
think about the ones who died.
When you become the one who gives out the certificates,
                                        orders, permission,
think about the ones who died.
When the little old lady comes to you with her problem,
                                        her little piece of land,
think about the ones who died.

See them without shirts, being dragged,
gushing blood, wearing hoods, blown to pieces,
submerged in tubs, getting electric shocks,
                                    their eyes gouged out,
            their throats cut, riddled with bullets,
    dumped along the side of the road,
                in holes they dug themselves,
                in mass graves,
or just lying on the ground, enriching the soil of wild plants:
You represent them.
The ones who died
delegated you.

TO COLONEL SANTOS LÓPEZ

Who'd ever tell you, Colonel,
when you were dying in Cuba from lung cancer,
       the FSLN still very far from any triumph,
that one day you would be exhumed from Cuba
and would triumphantly enter Managua
       (where you'd been only once before,
               the time they murdered Sandino)
cheered by a plaza of more than 100,000 people,
on the shoulders of the National Directorate
             and the Government's Junta,
      followed by all the ministers,
the Sandino flag waving everywhere,
      and the 21-cannon salute, and all that,
the entire country paying homage to Colonel Santos López,
the fatherless boy who worked ever since he was 8 years old,
               for 20 cents a day
    — the Yankees then masters of our homeland —
and you started fighting with Sandino at the age of 12
      in the squad of boys "the Choir of Angels,"
you didn't go to school,
      and later used to say
that because you didn't know how to read,
you had a clear mind for understanding intervention,

for which Commander Tirado now has called you
                "an intellectual even though he didn't write books
                        and an inexhaustible fountain of knowledge"
and you were wounded seven times,
                promoted by Sandino to Colonel,
and among the few who were at Sandino's midnight wedding
in San Rafael, pulling out of San Rafael that very night,
            with the General saying:
                        "From now on the linnets
                and all the birds will be the songs
that we'll have with us during our lives in the mountains,"
            a barefooted army, and barely clothed,
the leaves of plantain trees your bedding and blankets,
and Sandino called that poor troop
        the Defending Army of the National Sovereignty
                                        of Nicaragua,
            with all the diseases of the jungle
                and no more than medicines from the jungle itself,
only spells of relief, between this battle and that, at El Chipote
with guitars and accordions,
and the bombardments from airplanes, Sandino gave the order
        to shoot at the planes, that
first downed plane crashing in Quilalí,
there were your 216 battles,
                that time for instance, at the age of 18,
                when with Umanzor you stopped all the trains,

44

and at the end you accompanied Sandino on the fatal trip,
and were the only one who escaped in Managua,

                                   jumping from the roof,
going through a strange Nicaragua, with your wounded leg
all the way to Honduras, and starting to work there
              at the soap factory of Don Toribio, in Choluteca,
hidden always at the soap factory, the seemingly endless exile,
and 28 years later a young fellow, Carlos Fonseca, meets you,
       and you prove to be an envoy straight from Sandino,
the one who linked the first Sandinistas with the new breed
who right away informed you of the new struggle,
                 and you don't hesitate,
                       replying: "Let's go,"
and once again you are with the Choir of Angels,
founding the FSLN deep in the jungle on the banks
                                   of the Patuca River,
teaching vigilance, how to stand guard,
         how to move in the brush like a snake,
to carry the twig of a fluorescent tree at night
         so as not to get separated,
              to walk without leaving tracks,
to make ambushes the way Sandino would
                                   (three:
attacking the enemy in the middle
to finish them as they're running, in front or in back)
your fondness for "Tapir" because he was a peasant like you,

45

                    unable to read,
and your advice, the same as Sandino's,
            the peasants should continue to be our strength
backed by those who know more,
                the quarrel before you between Modesto and Francisco
                        for the command of a squadron
because Modesto wanted Francisco to be the leader and
                            Francisco wanted Modesto,
you fighting, old by now, once again on those rivers
                with cancer in your lung,
and later dying in a hospital in Cuba,
a death all alone, not engaged in battle, only the battle
                                with death,
                so far from any triumph,
when nobody knew when the triumph would be,
                        or if there'd be a triumph at all,
and now your return, cheered by an entire people,
who'd ever tell you, Colonel,
or maybe it wasn't necessary for anyone to tell you,
because when you were dying,
            who knows how, you already knew this,
            one way or another,
                who knows how,
                    you just knew everything.

THE PRICE OF BRAS

I have a niece who complains about the Revolution
because bras are so very expensive.
I don't know what it's like to have breasts
but I think I could go around without a bra.
My friend Rafael Cordova lives close to the village of Esquipulas
and he told me how many funerals used to pass on the road
                with tiny little coffins,
four, five, six, eight funerals
     every afternoon,
there were children's funerals,
                    each afternoon.
The old people didn't die as often.
And a short while ago the gravedigger of Esquipulas visited him:
"Doctor, I've come to ask you for a little help,
          I'm out of work.
          There aren't any funerals in Esquipulas anymore."
Before, bras were not so expensive.
Now in Esquipulas there are hardly any funerals.
You tell me: What's better?

THE STONE

From out of the earth came liquid magma
                    shot from the mouth of a volcano
             still burning red-hot
                              a river of red rock
             flowing downhill
a molten mass of sodium and silica
and it was cooling down, becoming solid, crystalizing,
        later separated from the rest of the mass
             the stone once lay beneath the sea
the sea receded and rivers washed it away
                         it rolled around some more on land
        finally it came to rest on a plain
its size being reduced little by little
by the rain, the sun and the wind
             smoothing it and making it almost round
                              its size smaller all the time
until one rainy September morning
when the filibusters attacked San Jacinto

Andrés Castro picked it up from the ground
and killed a Yankee with it.

(*Note:* The Battle of San Jacinto was the turning point in the
Filibuster War of 1855-57, in which the Nicaraguans defeated the
forces of William Walker, the father of U.S. military intervention in
Nicaragua.)

Their hot-pepper in typical foods
            — *khorovats*, Caucasian kebab —
                        just like jalapeño chili
— who influenced whom?
            The corn naturally comes from America.
                              In a field
(a cornfield out to the horizon)
        the high-tension rigs of the nuclear power-plant.

Big eyes and long eyelashes and bushy eyebrows.

         And the apricot that originated here
and that Alexander the Great . . . — But those two apricot faces:
An old woman and her two granddaughters with apricot faces,
the three talking back to an atheistic worker who
was yelling that God doesn't exist.
         "Or He let 2 million Armenians be massacred!"
I added: "He might be a God who can't do everything."
The man got angrier.

Then there was the boy from India
        who came to study for the priesthood here,
in the USSR.
He isn't a revolutionary, he told me, or a non-revolutionary
because in Calcutta there isn't a revolution.
        (His ever-ready smile of a new seminarian)

Next to a cuneiform inscription
                                a computer factory.

              Ancient
                      soviet socialist republic.
That it ran aground there
is an Armenian tradition as old as the hills.

MALTA

This is Malta.
Big ships in the harbor
   with black hulls and white tops,
as big as the fortifications near them,
and the fortress also thrusting its walls into the sea
        like ships' bows.
Yellow walls of the Knights of Malta.
    Ramparts
      built on ramparts.
  The Mediterranean:
blue turning white on the rocks.
     And huge round towers on top of these walls.
The sea was closed off here with a chain
when there were corsairs.
Old narrow streets over there
with lots of tv antennas
    Out to the horizon
the "wine-dark sea" according to Homer
— but does a blue wine exist?
      It's twelve different shades of blue.
Or where the blue turns into green and the green into foam.
Or:

Swells building up
      green with white
            striped-looking waves.
Beaches so clear you don't see water, just seaweed
on the bottom.
           Opposite Calypso's island
where Ulysses was held captive seven years.
       There weren't any tour guides then.
In a dark blue harbor
       fishing boats
with the eyes of Osiris painted on their bows
         near the yachts.
It's not the tourist season now.
The water is cold.
     In a grotto the blue
          fluorescent water
      where long ago sirens used to be seen.
And you still can easily think you're seeing them
when the sand on the bottom refracts the sunlight,
              making it rose- and
  mallow-colored.
But they only used to sing in the nighttime.
And you still can easily think you're hearing them
when the night wind is whistling through the cave.
     Pastel-colored houses.
       With flat rooftops against an arid background.

Saint Paul was shipwrecked here in 60 A.D.
maybe in front of that hotel.
The clover makes the March fields look pink.
      Sea glimpsed through a pine grove.
        Island of honey and roses, Cicero called it.
With hardly any soil, the ground mostly stones,
      the whole countryside crisscrossed by stone fences
and loaded with cactus which Columbus brought here.
Very close, behind Calypso's little island,
Pershing Missiles, on Sicily, menacing.
A little village below the cliffs
where there are simple restaurants.
        And right by the huge stone temple
          hot dogs.
Tiny island shaped like a fish
that all the empires have wanted for themselves,
Romans, Ottomans, Napoleon, Nelson, NATO:
free and at peace for the first time since the Phoenicians
now hosting an international meeting of pacifists and guerrillas
where I planted, for Nicaragua, an olive tree.

A MUSEUM IN KAMPUCHEA

We went into a museum that used to be a high school
but under Pol Pot the high school became
                the biggest prison in Cambodia.
The classrooms divided into little cells.
Here one only came to die.
More than 20,000 prisoners passed through here
                of whom only 17 survived,
the ones who hadn't yet been killed when the liberating
                                troops arrived.
                This was Pol Pot's "Democratic Kampuchea."
Here are the photos taken of them on entering.
                        They took photos of them all.
Some with their hands tied, others wearing chains
                                and iron collars.
        The worst thing to see was the horror in their faces.
You could see they weren't looking at the camera, but at death
                and the torture before death.
But even more shocking was a smiling face:
a girl, or teenage boy, someone innocent, unaware
evidently of what was going to happen to them.
        And photos of mothers with babies.
Some crude device for pulling out fingernails.
Tongs for tearing off nipples.

A great many different kinds of tools . . .
The tank where they were held underwater.
The posts where they were hanged.
The cell where Pol Pot's Minister of Information was also held
            before being killed.
More than 100 mass graves where they buried them
                                    have been found.
The infants buried with their milk bottles and pacifiers.
And the skulls, large piles of skulls
                that nobody wants to see.
        They killed 3 of the 8 million inhabitants.
They destroyed the factories, the schools, the medicines.
They'd jail someone for wearing glasses.
        The towns remained deserted.
The whole world knew about this.
How can it be that now, since Kampuchea was liberated,
the North American press doesn't speak badly of Pol Pot?
Finally we went outside.
                    There were flowers outside.
In a clean puddle a white duck fluttered
            bathing itself in the water and sun.
The young women who passed by on the street
looked like pagodas.

AMONG FACADES

We're going through the streets of a neighborhood in New York,
small shops, a restaurant, *Dry Cleaning*,
apartment houses, three-, four-stories high,
made of red brick, concrete, grey brick,
                    then we pass through a hamlet in the Alps,
            cobblestone streets in a Mexican village,
then a river with a medieval mill,
                a dusty street in a town in the West,
        with its saloons, a window with broken glass,
on a hill an 11th-century castle,
and once again apartment houses, a bank, liquor stores
        in any city in the United States,
but if you knock on anything, it sounds hollow,
                everything is plasterwork,
        they're only the outside walls, there's nothing in back.
A policeman in the middle of the street, with his badge
                and book for giving out tickets,
might be a real policeman or a famous actor.
And the producer (Ed Lewis) who is showing me everything
                                        tells me:
"no director, no producer, nobody
                runs the show in a movie,

just the bank putting up the money."
And on leaving and seeing the banks, restaurants, *Dry Cleaning*,
I thought whatever I'd knock on would sound hollow,
Hollywood, all of Los Angeles, everything
was merely walls
with nothing in back.

ROOM 5600

They had a happy childhood on the banks of the Hudson
on a 3500-acre estate
        with 11 mansions and 8 swimming pools
    and 1500 servants
        and a great house of toys
but when they grew up they moved into Room 5600
(actually the 55th and 56th floors of the tallest skyscraper
at Rockefeller Center)
where hundreds and hundreds of foundations and corporations
are managed like
        — what truly is —
      a single *fortune.*
Dependent on Room 5600 the millionaires in Venezuela
private enterprise in Brazil
       and you and I.
First there were ads in newspapers and on radios
                in Latin America
coming from that Room 5600
      ("a formative education for the young Rockefellers
in the vulnerabilities of the press")
all the programs involving the press divided into 2 categories
      "economic warfare" and "psychological warfare"
using news to make, explained Nelson to the Senate,

the same thing the military makes.
And Room 5600 used to have secret "observers"
            (kind of the first offspring of the present CIA)
providing information about owners, editorial politics,
personal opinions . . . even the least little reporter,
from which came their "propaganda analysis," dossiers
systematically organized on Latin American public opinion.
So in Room 5600
they learned the basics
of handling the news.
"They soon discovered that *news*
doesn't stem from facts
but from interest groups." And so that was how
the news about Latin America (edited in Washington)
            with economic incentives and economic pressures
reached Latin America from Room 5600
together with slick editorials, telephotos, flashes, "exclusive"
feature stories
            (and Walt Disney for the movies)
until 80% of the world news for Latin America
(originating in Washington)
was tightly controlled and monitored in New York
by Room 5600,
and so all the businesses in Latin America
(and its misery)
                        are linked to that Room 5600.

An operation that just required enough money
from Room 5600.
                    Our minds, our passions.
The thoughts of the lady who runs a boardinghouse.
                    The man walking some lonely beach.
A silhouette of lovers kissing in the moonlight
(influenced more by Room 5600 than by the moon)
Whatever Octavio Paz or Pablo Antonio Cuadra thinks.
Whether you say rose or say Russia
                    Room 5600 influences that.
                    Our perceptions conditioned by Room 5600.
And thousands of Latin American journalists
invited by Room 5600
 to Miami Beach where everything is fake, even the sea is fake,
a servile sea in front of your hotel.
And so
      NICARAGUA A TOTALITARIAN COUNTRY
THE SANDINISTAS ARE PERSECUTING THE CHURCH
                    MISKITOS MASSACRED
TERRORISTS . . .
That's why, American journalists, La Prensa is censored.
      Monopoly of what the public reads, hears, sees
as they fill the air with carbon monoxide, mercury, lead.
As for the press:
            "Silence was imposed on the poor"
Thanks to Nelson. To David, the younger one,

Chase Manhattan Bank
— "tied to almost every important business in the world" —
right in Room 5600
where the whole huge and scattered fortune
is only one fortune, there in one single Office.
With as many public-relations people in Room 5600
as they had servants in their childhood.
So their image changed from criminals to philanthropists.
        About whom, it is said, they did
everything, as with oil, with American politics,
except refining it.
        Corporations growing like a carcinoma.
And because of Room 5600
the holy family set up in garbage dumps.
Children playing by streams loaded with shit
        because of their monopolies.
Their monopolies that are getting fat on malnutrition.
Monopolies raising the price of the planet,
        bread and wine,
joys, medicines, *The Divine Comedy*.
Manhattan from offshore looking like a sacred mountain
and the seemingly heavenly skyscrapers raised
                                by the profiteering
in one of them:
        Room 5600, its lights Luciferian.
The shining waters of Lake Erie without fish

because of its sewers, the ones from Room 5600.

               Ducks drenched with oil.

Poison wind over deserts and dead rivers.

Contaminating the species with radioactive iodine

                                  Room 5600.

Manufacturing chocolates or napalm, it's the same to them.

And they manufacture *facts*.

At dusk you see from your car, above sulfurous bogs

the flickering fires of the oil refineries like Purgatory

and above them like a city in Oz

the glass skyscrapers lit up

      Wall Street and Rockefeller Center

with its Room 5600.

Every secretary of state since Dean Acheson

      that is, ever since I was 25 years old

has worked for a Rockefeller organization.

          "Do you remember those new companies

          coveted on the Stock Exchange like nubile girls?"

Their orgies with voluptuous and smiling bonuses

in Room 5600.

          "Does Rembrandt pay dividends?"

And the dividends from the Vietnam War.

       The profits from ESSO high as the stratosphere.

1 gallon of gas that cost the planet to produce it

1 million dollars . . .

      And Venezuela sold its oil for trinkets.

Twelve-year-old girls up for sale in the Northeast.
The cassava bread sour.
Sterilization of women in the Amazon.
Monopoly even of life itself.
The millions flowing to them as if in pipelines
owners of lands banks industries human beings
as if in pipelines from where the oilfields are huge
and the leases dirt-cheap.
They flooded New York with "moral bonds"
(that is, phony bonds)
Hence New York's bankruptcy
due to the billions in "moral bonds" from Room 5600.
Terrifying nations with cruel stories.
Its bat-like shadow over the culture, the academies.
All the weight of the presses on us.
Subjected to the whims of their stock companies.
That's why, Daniel Berrigan, Nicaragua's boys are fighting.
Whether milk or poison
the product doesn't matter
bread or napalm
the product doesn't matter.
David for instance had lunch with a Mr. Carter on Wall Street
and after lunch
he picked him to be President of the United States.
They continued their happy childhood
in Room 5600.

THE GUERRILLA'S WOMAN

She was the guerrilla's woman
        — even though the guerrilla was married —
and when he was killed she understood for the first time
what before she had heard but didn't understand:
        "the land holding the bones of our loved ones."
And since then she has loved this land much more
        though she already loved it a lot,
the land for which there are guards posted, battles fought.
Not only was it the land where she was born, the land of her life,
        now it was also the land of her dead one.
Last night when she was awakened for guard duty
she was dreaming that he was washing his clothes in the river,
on his naked chest bulged even the tiniest of his muscles.
She has a love buried in her heart
and some bones buried somewhere in this land.
This is one more reason for defending this land
against the Yankee invasion, against
        the contras,
because she was the guerrilla's woman.

THE U.S. CONGRESS APPROVES
AID TO THE CONTRAS

The senator sings out his speech in a baritone voice.
Beautifully modulated. Going up and down the scale
like someone playing an arpeggio on the trumpet,
                                    with frequent
runs,
            now it's a clarinet;
                    the long string of tangled words,
                        all their syllables exquisitely articulated,
        syl-la-bi-zing
skillfully the difficult passages of his bad prose
with the diction of a virtuoso.
The next speaker,
                        resonant language,
                            altiloquent and grandiloquent,
quoting long paragraphs of James Monroe from memory
as if reciting
                    without looking at the paper,
raising his voice (and his face)
                    and lowering it suddenly
to a deep bass.
            He sat down
all sweaty, acknowledging the halfhearted applause.

Bertilda washes her son's wounds,
and says: "Early in the morning I was going to make coffee
and I saw them beating up a kid in the street
and I cried 'Contras!' "
The boys began to shoot,
there were only two, and about a hundred contras.
The boys were her son and her nephew.
"So how did I feel? I didn't feel a thing, I just thought:
If they kill them they will have to kill me.
I loaded three clips for my nephew
because my boy was already wounded.
I put a rope on my two-year-old so she wouldn't run around."
Next:
a lively jumble of shifts in timbre and tone of voice,
with anastrophes,
prosopopoeias here and there, and clever paronomasias
and sonorous anaphoras.
His tropes resounding in the ornate chamber,
the ornamentation rebounding the grandiose echo;
few present at that moment in the chamber,
but spouting as if he were before a huge crowd
(hence the applause).
"Give yourselves up, you sons-of-bitches!"
yelled the guardsman.
"Let your mother give herself up!" replied Oscar Leonel
as if he were the other Leonel* reborn.

The small house destroyed
        by a lot of grenades and mortars.
The village desolated.
            The contras took off
leaving behind scattered propaganda about Christ.
        "Thirty million in humanitarian aid for the contras."
            "No sir, thirty-eight!"
            A high-pitched laugh from one of the humanitarians.
Another pounding the table, as if wanting to break it;
powerful gestures with both hands as if swinging a baseball bat;
"There is no problem of greater seriousness (slam)
saying this makes me shudder (slam)
than the threat (slam)
of Communism in Central America (slam)."
            "They killed my uncle,
his son Ramón too, they died fighting.
    Ramón's little boy, six years old,
was murdered in his bed.
He was asleep and they shot him.
He lay wounded and asked to see his dead father.
He put his hand on his face, and said: See,
                        they made a hole in him here.
    The little boy died right then too."
Thirty-eight million in humanitarian aid for the contras.

Dressed in pants, jacket and vest the color of night,
        with sharp incisor teeth,
                lips moving like a bloodsucker's
                        Vampyrum spectrum
    he sends out from his mouth and nostrils
similes, prolepsis, apostrophes,
                melodious alliterations,
repititions, entreaties, preteritions, digression,
        screeches from his wart-covered snout,
antithesis, synopsis, synonyms and antonyms.
And he seats himself. As if he were hanging upside down.
        Twisted tin roofs, burnt boards and posts.
What the cooperative had been.
Still smoking two days later.
On the hill
        the Catholic chapel was set on fire.
                And the little schoolhouse. The health center.
    Antibiotics in the ashes.
        And the buzzards gliding, gliding.
Fifteen-year-old Juan Antonio fought beside Estreberto,
                                aged 19.

A bullet in his chest
and he dropped on Estreberto's knees.
Some 30 contras grabbed Mario
and they slowly, ever so slowly, cut his throat,
     his blood spilling on the propaganda about Christ.
          The senator from Texas in a dramatic pose,
            his right foot forward,
    his arms opened out like a bronze statue,
as they bring him a glass of mineral water.
             Always the dramatic pose
        his left foot forward now;
   he is reading the speech that was written for him.
In the burnt out chapel, where the altar had been,
Estreberto stood: "Bitch, my poppa's blood is still here!"
No tears. Just squinting his eyes.
Estreberto saw when some 20 jumped Leonardo.
They stabbed him.
Juana said that she only saw the balls of fire.
She looked for little Enrique, three years old,
             and saw him sleeping.
     He was dead.
Loaded with the other kids, how could she carry him?
        "Not through those brambles, God help me!"
She left him in the brush, next to a stream.
             She laid a *bijagua* leaf
on him like a shroud.

With the slightly trembling voice of one holding back

deep emotions,

not reading, slowly reciting his speech:
"There is convincing proof (pause)
of an international Communist conspiracy (pause)
to export revolution (pause)
from Nicaragua (pause)
right up to our borders (pause)
and one of the . . .(pause) . . . in aid to the contras (pause)."
His arms shaking as if he were playing the piano.

A page brings him some ice-water.
One claw raised to ask for permission to speak.

The call to order.
The Honorable . . . . She had to leave him there
covered with just a little *bijagua* leaf.

They could hear the guardsmen laughing.
Lucía, so pretty, shot in the face.
Lidia they raped and dragged off.
The coffee beans, their small animals, their houses, everything.

"My housedress was soaked with the children's blood."

---

*Leonel Rugama: a 20-year-old poet and Sandinista fighter who was
killed in a shootout in 1970, and who died saying those words.

AT THE GRAVE OF A GUERRILLA

I think about your body that's been decomposing underground
making itself soft earth, humus once more
together with the humus of all the other humans
who have existed and will exist on our little globe
making all of us together fertile earth of our planet Earth.
And when the cosmonauts look at this blue and pink ball
                                        in the black night
what they will be seeing, far off, is your shining tomb
        (your tomb and the tomb of us all)
and when the beings from somewhere in outer space
                look at this dot of Earth's light
they will be seeing your tomb.
And one day it will all be a tomb, one silent tomb,
and there will no longer be any living beings on the planet,
                                        comrade.
        And then?
Then we will decompose more, we will fly, atoms in the cosmos.
And perhaps matter is eternal, brother
without beginning or end or it has an end and begins again
                                        each time.
Your love surely had a beginning but it has no end.
And your atoms that were in the soil of Nicaragua,

your loving atoms, that sacrificed themselves for love,
you'll see, they will turn into light,
I imagine your particles in the vastness of the cosmos

                                 like banners

like living posters.

              I don't know if I'm making myself clear.
What I do know is that your name will never be forgotten
and forever will be shouted: Present!

CITY LIGHTS PUBLICATIONS

Angulo, Jamie de. *JAIME IN TAOS*

Antler. *FACTORY (Pocket Poets #38)*

Artaud, Antonin. *ANTHOLOGY*

Bataille, Georges. *EROTISM: Death and Sensuality*

Baudelaire, Charles. *INTIMATE JOURNALS*

Bowles, Paul. *A HUNDRED CAMELS IN THE COURTYARD*

Breá, Juan & Mary Low. *RED SPANISH NOTEBOOK*

Brecht, Stefan. *POEMS (Pocket Poets #36)*

Broughton, James. *SEEING THE LIGHT*

Buckley, Lord. *HIPARAMA OF THE CLASSICS*

Buhle, Paul. *FREE SPIRITS: Annals of the Insurgent Imagination*

Bukowski, Charles. *THE MOST BEAUTIFUL WOMAN IN TOWN*

Bukowski, Charles. *NOTES OF A DIRTY OLD MAN*

Bukowski, Charles. *SHAKESPEARE NEVER DID THIS*

Bukowski, Charles. *TALES OF ORDINARY MADNESS*

Burroughs, William S. *ROOSEVELT AFTER INAUGURATION*

Burroughs, William S. *THE BURROUGHS FILE*

Burroughs, W.S. & Allen Ginsberg. *THE YAGE LETTERS*

Carrington, Leonora. *THE HEARING TRUMPET*

Cassady, Neal. *THE FIRST THIRD*

CITY LIGHTS JOURNAL No. 4

Codrescu, Andrei. *IN AMERICA'S SHOES*

Corso, Gregory. *GASOLINE/VESTAL LADY ON BRATTLE (Pocket Poets #8)*

David Neel, Alexandra. *SECRET ORAL TEACHINGS IN TIBETAN BUDDHIST SECTS*

Di Prima, Diane. *REVOLUTIONARY LETTERS*

Doolittle, Hilda. *(H.D.) NOTES ON THOUGHT & VISION*

Duncan, Isadora. *ISADORA SPEAKS*

Eberhardt, Isabelle. *THE OBLIVION SEEKERS*

Fenollosa, Ernest. *THE CHINESE WRITTEN CHARACTER AS A MEDIUM FOR POETRY*